LEAVING EGYPT BEHIND

MELONY BELL

ISBN 979-8-89043-486-9 (paperback)
ISBN 979-8-89043-487-6 (digital)

Christian Faith Publishing
832 Park Avenue
Meadville, PA 16335
www.christianfaithpublishing.com

Printed in the United States of America

Contents

Acknowledgments

I WOULD LIKE TO FIRST ACKNOWLEDGE the one who is my light and salvation—my Savior, Jesus Christ. I recognize that apart from Him, I am nothing, and I am forever grateful to partner with the Holy Spirit to write such an amazing book. He really is the author. I just said yes to writing down what He has asked me to share.

To my husband, Steven, I thank you for always supporting me and wanting nothing but the best for me. I look forward to forever with you.

To my daughter, Ziyan, my mini-me, I am so blessed to call you mine. You amaze me with your kindness, and I'm excited to see how God uses you.

To my son, Jaylon, I love you so much and know that God is equipping you for a major assignment. I can't wait to see you do amazing things for His kingdom.

To all who are reading this book, I pray that you discover what God has planned for your life. May you experience the fullness of life and heal from whatever has been holding you back from your Promised Land.

Introduction

IF YOU LIVE YOUR DAYS feeling broken, hurt, worrying, experiencing anxiety or anxiousness, feeling empty, unfulfilled, or wondering when you'll discover your god-given purpose this book is for you. Let me help you understand that the reason you feel the way you feel is because you have a uniqueness about you that God wants to use in the earth. But the enemy recognizes your greatness and has assigned an attack on your life. Overcoming Spiritual warfare is no easy feat but the good news is that you have power and authority over his weak tactics. I'm here to encourage you to fight for what God has promised you. Don't back down because what God has for you is worth fighting for. That's what this book is all about: discovering God at your burning bush and saying yes to living the life He has called you to. He has an assignment for you, but it will require you to "go back to Egypt" which represents your healing journey. We must go back to Egypt and deal with the things we've been avoiding and running from. Whether past mistakes, hurts, or abuse, God wants us to deal with these things so we can heal from them and begin receiving the promises of God in our lives. I call this our "Promised Land" and this book will help you to identify the issues that have kept you from living in your Promised Land. It will give you the tools and mindset to help you overcome those issues.

The truth is God transforms us but we don't need to be fully transformed before He decides to use us. To help you understand this, we'll be analyzing the story of Moses leading the Israelites out of Egypt in the book of Exodus. My goal is to speak to you prophetically and help you gain revelation into the processes God often uses when He transforms us through our healing journey. Moses had deep rooted issues but He was no doubt called by God to complete an amazing task: leading the Israelites out of Egypt into the Promised Land. No matter the excuses Moses gave God, God still used Him and the same is true for us. What excuses do you have as to why you cannot accept God's promises in your life and fight for what is rightfully yours? You don't need to be fully transformed (if there is such a thing) before God begins to use you. In fact, the transformation process begins with you saying yes to God and continues through your following His instructions.

It is true that God wants us to live in harmony with Him and He wants to bless us in such a way that we would acknowledge only He could have done it for us. He is a Father, the best Father you could ever have and any Father would want to see his children healed, delivered, and living the best life possible. He also acknowledges that if we don't heal, we'll pass down brokenness to our children and the cycle will continue to repeat itself. Today is the day we must be intentional and choose inner healing so we don't continue to be distracted from our assignment and purpose on earth. Will you say "yes" to your healing journey today? Will you refuse to let the enemy devour you or your family any longer? Will you let go of fighting God and having control and let Him guide you?

The truth is we are all special and unique in God's eyes. No matter what stage of life you're in, God will take you from your Egypt, through your wilderness, and into your Promised Land. Once God equips us with wisdom and understanding, we can become more confident in our calling, living out God's purpose for us. It is extremely important that you let God use you because your story, your testimony, your experience is crucial to the Kingdom of God. Yes, I said it, you are important to the Kingdom of God and your role is a major one. As we navigate through leaving our Egypt into the Promises of God, it is my prayer that you will let go and let God. No matter what abuse you've experienced - the divorce, the hate, the drugs, promiscuity, or the baby out of wedlock, God can use it all. Won't you let go of your Egypt today?

Fear: The Number One Tactic

*So the Egyptians made the Israelites their slaves. They
appointed brutal slave drivers over them, hoping to wear them
down with crushing labor. They forced them to build the cities
of Pithom and Rameses as supply centers for the king.*
—Ex 1:11 (NLT)

Extremely powerful

THE BOOK OF EXODUS BEGINS where the book of Genesis
left off. Joseph, son of Jacob (a.k.a. Israel), had favor with Pharaoh,
so Pharaoh allowed Joseph to move his father and all his brothers
to the best land of Egypt (Gn 47:11). But eventually, Joseph,
Jacob, and all his brothers died, ending that entire generation, and
a new pharaoh rose to power (Ex 1:6). However, the Israelites (the
descendants of Jacob) had many children and grandchildren and
became *extremely powerful*. Wait a minute, *extremely powerful*? Are
we talking about the same Israelites that the Egyptians forced to
become slaves (Ex 1:11)? How is it that they were so powerful,
yet the Egyptians were able to easily instill fear in them and force
them into slavery?

Chapter 1 in the book of Exodus reveals to us that when
we don't know who we are or whose we are, fear will enslave us.

Can you recognize this in your life right now? You find fear has somehow crept into your life, and you're unable to start the business you've been talking about for ten years. Maybe your immediate response is to agree with me and thank God that you are not like the Israelites, who so foolishly let the enemy trick them into slavery. But before you celebrate, take a moment and think about where you are and if there is a bit of "Egypt" in you that you need God to help you dispose of. No matter how far behind or far ahead in life you feel you are, fear can find a way to paralyze you if you do not fully understand whom you belong to. The Israelites were a blessed people. They were extremely powerful, and God favored them. They literally had God himself to help them fight their battles. But somewhere along the way, the people of Israel forgot how to call on God when they needed help. They were not living the life God had designed for them.

What do you believe?

Until you can recognize the truth of who you are in Christ, fear will continue to paralyze you. It is time to expose the fear in your life so God can strengthen you in this area. The Bible says you were bought with a high price (1 Cor 6:20). You were bought with the blood of Jesus Christ, and you belong to God. Just like the Israelites, you are extremely powerful with the ability to overthrow the Egyptians in your life because they are outnumbered and have no authority over God's people (Ex 1:9). Do you believe in your heart that you are extremely powerful? Do you believe in your heart that God has given you power and authority (Lk 10:19)? Do you believe in your heart that God has major plans for your life? Do you believe in your heart that God can and wants to use you?

Notice I said the phrase "Do you believe in your heart," not "If you know in your mind." Knowing something is completely different from believing it. Yes, faith (or believing) comes by hearing, and hearing by the Word of God (Rom 10:17), but many people settle for what they hear or know. We spend hours watching informational YouTube videos, reading books, and studying to take tests. We soak up so much information, but we often miss spending time working on what we believe. How catastrophic it is when we spend no time cultivating our beliefs when our beliefs are what govern our lives. If you don't understand the severity of your beliefs, read Romans 10:10, and you'll discover that your very salvation depends on what you believe.

Most often it is extremely painful for us to look at where we are in life and ask ourselves the right questions to determine how we got there. But I believe that if we acknowledge that we've been ignoring our beliefs and start working on them, we'll see radical change in our lives. You might have let fear paralyze you for the last thirty years, but at any point, you can let go of that fear and move into the promises of God. But until you recognize and acknowledge the problem in your life, I can assure you nothing will change. Begin to let the pain of not living the fulfilled life you desire hurt worse than where you currently are.

Whom will you fear?

Fear certainly has its place, but it's up to us to decide what or who we will fear. Pharaoh, the king of Egypt, ordered the Hebrew midwives to kill any boys the Israelites birthed. The midwives feared God and instead allowed the Israelite baby boys to live (Ex 1:17). Their fear of the Lord blessed them as God gave them families of their own. When we fear things or people more than we fear God, the result is slavery. But when we fear God more, we are actually saying we revere Him (Phil 2:12). We stay away from evil, and we live our lives to please God. May I remind you that God has not given us a spirit of fear but of power, love, and a sound mind (1 Tm 1:7)? By now I hope you're starting to recognize that the paralysis in your life comes from fear. So how can you make the changes that will put you on the right track to exiting Egypt and entering the Promised

Land? I've mentioned a few key points already, but here is a list of things you can implement in your life now:

- *Get tired of the pain.* Living in pain is not God's desire for you. Begin to get so fed up with what or who is causing you pain that you raise the white flag up to God as an act of surrender.
- *Surrender.* Allow Him full access to your life. I'll be honest here and say that when I got serious about my walk with God, I partially surrendered. I can't say I completely trusted God with my life, but I was willing to move in the right direction. Don't feel bad if you feel like you just can't let go; God has a keen ability to recognize what He needs to do in your life to gain your trust. You just need to surrender your heart and let God do the rest.
- *Give God what you have.* It's okay to be afraid. Just don't stay there. Sometimes we are just flat-out scared of giving God our lives because it means change. We must let go of what we are familiar with and enter new territory. The good news is that it's God's territory, and He's the Master of it. Additionally, we are often alone, with no one in our lives to help guide us; so when we are finally ready to surrender to God, we feel that we don't have much to offer. God is fond of leftovers. He delights in taking what people call trash and turning it into beautiful treasure.
- *Take one step at a time.* Focus on what's in front of you. Ask God what it is you need to do right now and do it. Don't allow excuses to come out of your mouth. Get moving and do what God is asking you to do. Whenever my daughter, Ziyan, is afraid of doing something, my husband, Steven, often tells her, "Do it scared."
- *Put God over everything.* It baffles me that we hustle and bustle, then complain to God that we are tired of our situation, yet we don't let God bring us the very relief we're looking for. He is the Author of life, but He will

not force His will on you. If you are too busy for God, then don't expect your situation to change. You need to halt all efforts and get to the root cause of the issue, and that may be your lack of attention to God. You don't need to spend three hours with Him every day. He just wants your heart. Begin with ten uninterrupted minutes every day with God. Worship, read Scripture, pray, cry, do what you need to do to put Him first.

- *Get practical.* I'm a firm believer that God made us spiritual but practical. Earlier we talked about cultivating our beliefs. Affirmations are very helpful in this area. Take a postcard and write down a promise from the Bible or something you need to work on believing, then recite it for ten minutes every day. There are so many things I can say about being practical, but they are outside the scope of this book. Do some research on how you can be more practical in an area you need to improve.

Testimony time

There was a time in my life where I didn't realize how powerful I was. Naturally, I am a quiet and reserved person, which makes me a target for bullies. I was molested as a young child in elementary school. Because it was swept under the rug, I grew up confused about sex and God's design for it. That quickly resulted in watching pornography and promiscuous behavior. There was a time in my life when I desperately wanted love, so I jumped from relationship to relationship, looking for something only God could give me. The result was being bullied and used by different men who, in their defense, were just as broken as I was. It is true that hurt people hurt people! It was the empty feeling I could no longer take. I knew it was time to stop clinging to sin and cling to God. What's interesting about my situation is that I knew God was up to something. I knew my life had greater purpose, so one of the first things I began praying for was wisdom. I was tired of being trapped in my mind, so I pleaded with God to pour out His wisdom in me.

He wasted no time. God began to show me what a powerhouse I was. I discovered I had the ability to call down heaven through prayer, praise, and worship. He began speaking to me through dreams, and I soon discovered my prophetic ability. I had spent my whole life living in fear, but when I discovered who I was in Christ, it made sense why the enemy attacked me so strongly. He was afraid I'd discover whom I belonged to.

I am happy to say that fear no longer paralyzes me! I have spent so much time with God that I've come to understand that nothing can limit Him. He has a call in my life, and although I get scared or anxious sometimes, I quickly remind myself of whom I belong to. I have learned to fight for God's promises, which has inspired me to share with you what I've learned along my journey. It is my assignment, and I will not let the devil rob me of it. I can truly say I'll never back down from a challenge. I know that if God tells me to do something, I am fully equipped, and I don't have to do it with my own strength. I pray that as we continue to navigate this book, you learn to fight for what is rightfully yours.

Chapter **2**

Strong and Weak

*God heard their groaning, and he remembered his covenant
promise to Abraham, Isaac, and Jacob. He looked down
on the people of Israel and knew it was time to act.*

—Ex 2:24–25 (NLT)

We need God's strength

CHAPTER 2 OF EXODUS BEGINS with the story behind Moses's birth, his fleeing from Egypt to Midian, and the birth of his children. Moses was born of parents from the tribe of Levi; he was a natural-born Israelite and rightfully a child of God (Ex 2:2). But he was born during a time where the Israelites were in great pain because of the hardship of slavery. Moses's life was at risk from the moment he was born because he was an Israelite boy and Pharaoh had it out for the Israelites.

May I remind you that from the moment you are born, Satan can recognize that you are a child of God. Just as God has plans for your life, so, too, does the enemy. I heard my pastor say that one of the greatest strengths of the devil is that he can see the future. The devil can often recognize your potential before you can. That's why he is after our children. If he can distract their minds from a young age, he can keep them from ever thinking about whom they belong to.

If we are not careful, we'll look up and recognize the injustices in our world before we recognize God. When this happens, we begin to focus our attention on police brutality, racism, a broken justice system, and everything else that's wrong with the world. We are ready to speak our minds on Twitter, talk about how we feel, and say what we think, but we leave God out of it.

Before you get offended, in no way am I saying it's wrong to speak up when you see injustices. In fact, I strongly believe we should speak up when we see our brothers or sisters being mistreated. But if our speech is filled with hate and all we do is talk about what's wrong, we are actually being distracted by the enemy. We contribute to more chaos, cussing each other out, fighting, and looting, but never do we consult God and ask what we should be doing. We think we're making progress by speaking up, but if we don't have God's direction or approval on something, the progress we see is temporary. Only God can produce lasting change. There are many other ways the enemy distracts us including lust, drugs, alcohol, social media, music, etc. Beware that you are not building your foundation on a distraction from the enemy. He is a master manipulator, and what you think you may be accomplishing is nothing if God has not ordained it for you.

Moses was deeply troubled by the Egyptian beating the Hebrew slave (Ex 2:11). There was no doubt Moses's heart hurt for the poor Hebrew slave. Even though Moses didn't grow up as a slave, he still had compassion for his people. But instead of Moses consulting God about what needed to be done, he took matters into his own hands and killed the Egyptian. When we take matters into our own hands, the result is sin. When we sin, the result is often shame, guilt, and running from what God wants for us. Moses had to flee Midian because the news of his killing the Egyptian reached Pharaoh. Pharaoh wanted Moses's life in exchange for the Egyptian's. Moses now had to go through a period of living as a foreigner before he realized what God wanted him to do. As a child of God, you are no doubt strong. But the people of God need a reminder that God is not looking for strength. He's looking for those who recognize we are weak apart from Him.

Paul so eloquently reminds us about this when he said he begged God to take away the thorn in his flesh but was instead told by God that His power worked best in weakness (2 Cor 12:8–10).

God never quits on you

The good news is that God never quits on us. No matter how far gone you may feel, God is always willing to take you in. He has an assignment for you, and He is well aware of all your past mistakes and hurts. He knew you would make those mistakes before they happened. Be encouraged! God has enough grace to cover your transgressions. It doesn't matter what you did or who hurt you. God loves you and wants you more than ever. If you are struggling with accepting that God loves you and wants to use you, I encourage you to read Romans 8. It reminds us that nothing can separate us from God's love.

> Neither death nor life, neither angels nor demons, neither our fears for today nor our worries about tomorrow—not even the powers of hell can separate us from God's love. (Rom 8:38)

God surely didn't quit on Moses. Murder did not stop God from seeing how He could use Moses to bring relief to the Israelites. In fact, I believe God's hand was on Moses's life in the midst of him dealing with Pharaoh trying to kill him. He found favor with Reuel, a citizen of the land of Midian. Reuel became his father-in-law and gave Moses his daughter Zipporah to be his wife (Ex 2:21). Moses and Zipporah also gave birth to a son. Indeed, in the midst of trouble, God blessed Moses with a place of safety and a family of his own. That is often true for us, especially when we are living in sin. God shows us love and tender mercy even in our disobedience. It is not His approval of sin but His approval of us. And though He showers us with grace, we should not continue sinning to receive that grace (Rom 6:1).

Testimony time

When I think about the love of God, I want to burst out crying like a little baby. His love overwhelms me, and I feel like I'm going to explode. There was a time in my life when I felt worthless, a big nothing. I have to fight back tears when I think of how low my self-esteem was and how God delivered me from it. Just like Paul, I take pride in my weaknesses because I know it's at that moment where I feel I've had enough that God is in full control. I am strong but weak. I used to run myself to the ground, trying to survive. Now, whenever I have a problem, I cry to my Father in surrender. He comforts me every time, and I can feel Him reminding me that He will not let my pain go to waste. He reminds me that pain is necessary for my growth. If I am strong all the time, I'll never need God. God loves us so much that He doesn't want a moment away from us. He allows pain in our life because pain causes us to fully lean on Him. Will you surrender to God today? Will you trust Him with your life? Will you no longer accept the lies of the enemy and consult God about the truth?

Chapter 3

Equipped for the Assignment

But Moses protested to God, "Who am I to appear before Pharaoh? Who am I to lead the people of Israel out of Egypt?"
—Ex 3:11 (NLT)

Encountering God

BEFORE GOD ASKED MOSES TO approach Pharaoh and tell him to free the Israelites, He performed a miracle. We are all familiar with the burning bush. Moses gazed at it in amazement because the bush was engulfed in flames, yet it did not consume the bush (Ex 3:3). Fast-forward, and God and Moses are becoming acquainted, and God lays it on Moses: "Now go, for I am sending you to Pharaoh. You must lead my people Israel out of Egypt" (Ex 3:10). Moses had spent the last forty years in Midian. Can you imagine how Moses must have felt? No doubt he was thinking, *Lord, Egypt is my past. I have been delivered from it, and there is no need to go back.* When God has an assignment for you, there are two things you can count on: experiencing His divine presence and having to confront your past. Sometimes we think that because years have passed, we're delivered from our hurt. Then God asks us to dive deep, and we quickly realize we've just put a Band-Aid on the pain.

If you think there is no purpose in thinking about the past, you are sadly mistaken. Where else do testimonies live? By God's grace, we'll have future testimonies, but it's the ones we can share now that will impact lives. The longer we go without addressing our past hurts or mistakes, the harder it becomes to deal with them. It's like trying to treat an infected wound. Had we treated it sooner, we could have prevented the infection and begun the healing process. The good news is that God is a divine healer, and He knows exactly what you need. The healing process begins when you say yes to God. And though it is hard initially, it gets easier to deal with the pain after a while. You can take comfort in knowing that God will never leave you or forsake you (Heb 13:5). You are not alone.

Be open-minded to the help God is trying to give you. One of the biggest mistakes we can make is saying no to getting help through counseling. We expect God to just heal us, but the truth is that without the help of those who've overcome the same obstacles, it is nearly impossible to heal. It's like trying to treat that infected wound without the help of a doctor. When we get help through counseling, we get a different perspective on our situation. Sometimes we're so buried in hurt and can't hear from God, so He will speak through the people He has assigned to help us. The point is that you need to talk to someone with spiritual maturity and wisdom, someone who will not judge and is genuinely trying to help you.

Maybe you are thinking, *I'm a doctor and can treat my own infection.* You may be a professional at helping others, but when we try to treat our own wounds, we lose objectivity. You are too close to home and too vulnerable to clearly see all aspects. It's also okay to need the help of others. You are not weak because you need help. In fact, when you are able to quickly identify that you need someone's help, you free your mind of the worry of resolving the issue by yourself. You can now focus on resolution and not troubleshooting; you leave the troubleshooting to the professional. Remember, even Jesus had the help of twelve disciples. If God can get the help of others, so can you.

Fully equipped

God does not ask us to do something without having equipped us for the mission. Moses protested to God, saying, "Who am I to appear before Pharaoh? Who am I to lead the people of Israel out of Egypt?" (Ex 3:11). Moses evidently did not understand who he was dealing with. God had to tell Moses, "I AM WHO I AM" (Ex 3:14). So many of us are dealing with exactly what Moses dealt with. We feel we aren't good enough to be blessed or carry out the assignment. We somewhat understand how powerful and mighty God is and that He can do all things. Then we look at the testimonies of others and think, *God has done it for them, but He won't do it for me.* Today I prophetically declare that you are going to gain a divine perspective on what it means to be fully equipped! Let's look at some of the things you are already equipped with:

- *Divine presence.* First and foremost, you're equipped with the help of God. Just like with Moses, God is reminding you that not only is He going back to Egypt with you, but He will also give you a sign that He is the one who sent you (Ex 3:12). God did not tell Moses to go back to Egypt and figure out how to get the people out. He didn't say, "I'll bless you, then I'll be waiting for you out in the wilderness whenever you accomplish the mission." No, He said, *"I'll be with you."* Don't let the enemy trick you into thinking you are alone. God has equipped you with His divine presence and help.
- *Pain.* Your pain qualifies you to be used by God. Jesus told us He came for the sick, not those who think they are righteous (Mk 2:17). How can we be used to help the sick if we haven't experienced pain and the healing of that pain through a relationship with Christ?
- *Favor.* God told Moses that He would give Him favor with the Egyptians (Ex 3:21). Many of us have heard over and over that we are highly favored, yet we don't feel God's favor. It's likely that we are confusing *favor* with

favorite. Favor doesn't mean you'll have a pain-free life; it means you have God's approval.

- *Insider information.* God may not give you the how but most likely will give you the what. This is awesome news! Don't allow the disappointment of not knowing how overshadow the excitement of the what. I know, I know. Sometimes we are terrified of the what, just like Moses. But God gave Moses some juicy details of what was to come (Ex 3:18–22). God will give you glimpses into your future and what is to come. Take comfort in knowing you aren't blindly walking into something because your Father has already worked it out.

- *Direction.* God certainly gave Moses a lot of instructions. At the first glimpse, it may seem overwhelming how much instruction Moses received, but God wanted to make sure Moses knew exactly what he needed to do. You will never have to go back to Egypt without some guidance and direction from God. Open your heart and your spiritual ears and follow the instructions that God is giving you.

Ask questions

I want to emphasize that it's okay to ask God questions. Though we can learn from Moses's "mistakes," we can't judge his actions. He had questions for God, and he wasn't afraid to ask them. I encourage you to ask God questions when you don't understand. I'm not saying that He will give you all the answers, but His response will be what you need to get going. Listen, God is the Alpha and the Omega, and He is the first and the last as well as the beginning and the end (Rv 22:13). If you don't have questions for Him, something is wrong. We're human, which means we can never fully understand the depth of God's ways. So when He asks us to do something, our natural eye looks around and can't make sense of it. Our first thought is *But how?* Ask God the questions you need and count it as joy because if you're asking God how, it means He has spoken to you and wants to use you.

Testimony time

I'll be the first to say that sometimes, when God asks me to do something, it can be a bit intimidating, and I start to question Him. The first experience that comes to mind is when God told me to sign up for the Ministers in Training (MIT) program at my church to become an ordained minister. This was around December 2019, right before the coronavirus pandemic. At the time, I was a single mother of two and working a full-time job. When I first heard God speak to me about MIT, I quickly dismissed it, saying, "Surely, God doesn't want me to go through such a rigorous program. I'd be away from my children." I also live in the Atlanta area, and we are infamously known for our horrific traffic. The thought of having to commute weekly made me dread having to join the program. It made absolutely no sense to me. I knew the program was demanding, and I just could not understand why God would want me to do such a thing. I also dreaded the thought of going back to school after having earned my master's degree and becoming a certified public accountant (CPA). I thought, *This could not be God.*

Can you guess what happened next? Yup, God was persistent and did not let it go. I would hear MIT advertised on our Sunday-morning announcements and felt convicted. He would interrupt my thoughts and tell me what I was going to do in the future. He would not let it go, so I knew I was going to lose the fight with God. I comforted myself with the reality that even though I didn't understand, it would all work out because God was my present help. I was obedient and signed up for the program. I immediately saw the hand of God move and was quickly accepted into the program. Every piece came together smoothly and effortlessly, so I knew it was God. I still had my questions, but all I could do was wait until the program started and take it day by day.

February of 2020 came, and it was time to start the program. I had prepared as much as I could for this new journey that would take two years to get through. But then it happened. Coronavirus spread, and it was time to go on lockdown. I certainly feel the pain of those who've lost loved ones during the pandemic and am in no way dismissing the grief that resulted from the pandemic. I can say, however, that during this scary time, I quickly realized that God had planned for me to go through MIT during the pandemic. Traffic was no longer a concern since all my classes were online. Being away from my children was no problem since I'd gotten an overdose of time with them by being on lockdown. My questions were answered, and I was glad I said yes to God.

I also quickly learned that God had plans to take me back to my Egypt. I had spent the last year of my life abstaining from sex and filling up on God, so I thought I was completely healed from my past hurts and relationships. I'd soon learn that was not true since the enemy began to send attacks my way because I was on a mission for God. But because my heart was so on fire for the Lord, I was determined not to let my struggle or triggers take me back to a life I vowed to never relive. I reached out to the leaders of the MIT program and was able to begin working with a Christian counselor. The rest is history. I went on to learn about how the enemy attacked me through my mindset, and today I am stronger than ever. I have been in situations where I just could not see what God was trying to accomplish in my life. There are times I have been so overwhelmed as a leader that I have pleaded with God to give me a break from leading. When this happens, it is time to remind myself that He is a sovereign God. Don't let your fear of the past or your present situation keep you from saying yes to God. It's time to go back to Egypt.

Chapter 4

Stumbling Blocks

*But Moses pleaded with the Lord, "O Lord, I'm not very good
with words. I never have been, and I'm not now, even though you
have spoken to me. I get tongue-tied, and my words get tangled."*
—Ex 4:10 (NLT)

Negative opinions

MOSES MADE SOME VALID POINTS with the Lord when he
tried to talk his way out of going back to Egypt. Initially, he focused
on the Israelites not believing God had sent him to deliver them
from Egypt. But as God easily dismissed the idea by performing
signs and wonders, Moses had to cling to something else. It was
evident to Moses that God was all-powerful and could get the
Israelites to believe. So he shifted his focus to his limiting beliefs.

Our limiting beliefs are sometimes birthed out of the negative opinions of others. Moses wanted God to send someone else
because he believed he was not cut out for the assignment (Ex
4:13). Somewhere along the way, someone must have told Moses
he had a speech problem and probably made fun of him. I bet
if you asked the people of Midian if he could do what God was
asking, they'd say no. Negative opinions can cripple us if we're
not careful. The negative opinions from others don't come from

a healthy place. Whenever someone shares their negative opinion of you, take a moment to be quiet and ask yourself a few questions before you take in what they've said. Are they living a godly life and have a heart for God? Are they genuine? Are they dealing with past hurts they need healing from? Do you admire the way this person lives? Does what they said resonate with your spirit as if it is confirmation from the Holy Spirit? If you've said no to these questions, then you're probably dealing with someone who is projecting their hurt onto you.

I want to take a moment and recognize that sometimes those negative opinions come from those closest to us, like a mother or father, a spouse, a sibling, or a best friend. It's those we love the most, who we crave attention from, that can really hurt us. And because they have a special place in our hearts, we see their opinions as law and live by them. Please recognize that the ones we love most are human. They, too, have a story as well as past hurts and pain that, if not healed from, will continue to be passed down from generation to generation. That's what a generational curse is—habits and cycles that we continue to repeat. If this resonates in your spirit, it is likely that God has called you to end the cycle. This is your assignment! He recognizes the abuse that keeps happening in your bloodline. He wants you to be the first to change things—the one to live a life of obedience, heal, and pave the way for future generations. It's hard overcoming hurt from people we love most, but remember that God will never leave or forsake you. He will never treat you harshly; and He has nothing but grace, love, and mercy to give.

Thankfully, God does not consider opinions when choosing your assignment! He is a sovereign Lord and knows exactly who or what He needs. Indeed, God could have chosen anyone to deliver the Israelites, but it was Moses God wanted to use. Many of us are like Moses, giving God excuses and telling Him to use someone else. God doesn't want to use someone else; He wants to use you. You're unique, and the Father recognizes this. Let this comfort you because you are special to God. Don't let what you feel is a weakness overshadow God's ability to use you. It's okay to recognize where you fall short, but take pride in the fact that God is your strength. Can we take a moment to soak that in? God is your strength! I don't know about you, but if I have the Almighty on my side, surely, I will win the fight! There is no losing when you have God! Recognize the hand of God in your life. Don't wait for a burning bush before you get moving. God doesn't need you to be perfect; He has already sent a perfect Savior on your behalf.

The Holy Spirit

God decided to let Moses's brother Aaron go with him on his journey back to Egypt (Ex 4:16). I believe this is symbolic to the role of the Holy Spirit in our lives. The Holy Spirit is our advocate. He is our teacher and reminds us of God's Word (Jn 14:16). He is your mouthpiece, just as Aaron was to Moses. He instructs you on what to say and is your internal GPS system, giving you direction and clarity. I cannot stress enough the importance of the Spirit in our lives. If you are having a hard time hearing from God or just want to hear His voice more, then it starts with His spirit. Whether you're on your way back to Egypt or on your way to the Promised Land, you will need His direction. You are never alone because the Spirit lives in you. Begin to develop hearing God's voice and receiving His direction now. Here are a few things to consider when developing in this area:

- *Bible study.* Knowing the Word is crucial to hearing God's voice. The enemy comes to steal, kill, and destroy, and it's easy for him to do so when you lack knowledge of God's Word (Hos 4:6). Commit to reading God's Word regularly so you become acquainted with His Word and can discern between His voice and the voice of the enemy.
- *Prayer.* The Holy Spirit is attracted to prayer. When you begin to pray, He begins to move. Pray whenever you can and get serious about it. If you feel dry in your prayer life, start with gratitude. Begin to meditate on the things God

has done for you and what He's either already brought you out of or promised to bring you through.

- *Praise and worship.* There is nothing like a good worship song. It sings to our hearts and, at the same time, brings glory and honor to our Lord. Build your playlist of worship music. You may find that in moments of worship, you suddenly hear God's voice and receive divine direction.
- *Prophetic training.* I caution you in the area of prophetic ministry. There are a lot of people who claim to hear from God and say some bizarre things. There are also people who have the best intentions but lack the wisdom to speak to the hearts of people and end up causing more harm than good. Nevertheless, I have found it beneficial to be around prophetic people. Find a properly trained prophetic group that has a heart for Jesus and seeks to build others up. Being around people like this will help you increase your ability to hear God's voice.

Who's on your side?

It is a beautiful thing to have the Lord with you at all times. However, we must recognize the importance of having others help us along our journey. We see this in Moses and Aaron performing miracles for the elders of Israel (Ex 4:30). God could have had Moses and Aaron go directly to Pharaoh and cut to the chase, but he had them approach the elders first. God will often send us to those we need support from, or He'll send them to us. Either way, God wants to surround us with people we can worship with—those who carry the same vision and can encourage us to keep fighting. For some of us, having people surround us is a foreign concept, but we'll discuss the issues we may have with people in the next chapter.

Final thoughts

Acts 7:22 says Moses was powerful in both speech and action. Are we talking about the same Moses who pleaded with the Lord not to send Him to Egypt because He would get tongue-tied (Ex 4:10)? That's the power of the Spirit in our lives. If we allow Him, He takes full control, and we accomplish amazing things we could not do on our own. Our faith begins to increase because we see Him moving. Out of our mouths comes wisdom from the mind of God. We gain divine perspective and begin to own the power and authority God has given us. Furthermore, we soon realize we don't need to be experts in what God has called us to do. We just need to get started, and we'll learn along the journey.

Testimony time

In my walk with Christ, I realized that everything He's had me do is bigger than just me. The decisions I make, the people I interact with, and the things I say all lead back to my family. My bloodline has struggled with alcoholism, pornography, promiscuity, and poverty. But God has called me to be the catalyst of change for my family. Before I could break the cycle, however, God had to work on my heart. He took me back to my Egypt, where I had to forgive those who've wronged me. I had to let go of the hate I had for people I let close to my heart. I had to forgive some of my family members for their shortcomings. I can admit that it hurt. When you have been beaten down and abused by people you love, it can be hard to overcome if you don't first give it to God and also learn how to fight for freedom. I had to learn to forgive myself for all the things I did to grieve the Holy Spirit. God had to take away all the shame and guilt of my past mistakes and replace it with joy and peace. That joy and peace now allow me to be the godly wife and mother that God has called me to be. I am able to educate my children about generational curses and teach them to rise above all the mistakes I've made. I pour back into them and continuously seek God's direction on how to best lead them. I can sleep at night knowing that I've broken the cycle and that by the blood of Jesus, all assignments or plots of the enemy are canceled. As for me and my house, we will serve the Lord (Jo 24:15).

I have also learned the importance of the Holy Spirit in my life. I commune with him often, and whenever He speaks, I listen. He gives me glimpses of my future. He keeps me in check when I get full of myself. He gives me direction and peace as confirmation when I'm on the right road. He shows me the gifts and talents my children possess and convicts me if I'm too harsh on them. He gives me clarity, and He's the very reason I am able to write this book. I make room for Him to pour out His wisdom and knowledge and ask Him how I can use that to help others. I can truly say that without Him, I would be nothing and not be sharing my story with you. But most importantly, when I start feeling like I can't do something or am not cut out for the assignment, He gives me the push I need to keep going. He reminds me that I can do all things through Christ, who is my strength (Phil 4:13).

Chapter **5**

False Accusations

*But Pharaoh shouted, "You're just lazy! Lazy! That's why
you're saying, 'Let us go and offer sacrifices to the Lord.'"*
—Ex 5:17 (NLT)

Who are you?

WE CONTINUE WITH EXODUS 5, where Moses and Aaron are now carrying out God's instruction to approach Pharaoh (Ex 5:1). Moses is now back in Egypt, the place he fled because he killed an Egyptian. It is a scary place, but Moses has encountered God and is well equipped for the journey. God has already proven Himself to Moses and assured him that He'll never leave his side. At this point, there is no denying that this is a God-ordained assignment for Moses. Yet Pharaoh quickly dismisses the idea of letting the Israelites go offer sacrifices to God and even accuses them of being lazy (Ex 5:8). If you think you will carry out the assignment of God with no opposition from Satan, then let this story bring you a revelation. It is guaranteed to happen! The enemy is afraid of your potential in Christ, and it's a threat to the kingdom of darkness. Satan works night and day to stop you with fear, lies, and accusations (1 Pt 5:8). We must be aware of his tactics, or else we'll find ourselves back in Egypt. And instead of fulfilling the assignment, we run away. How tragic it would have been for Moses to flee back to Midian because he faced opposition.

This is all too familiar to some of us. We've been accused and abused all our lives. We've been called liars, thieves, and no good and told we'd never amount to anything. This is a plot against your destiny and does not come from God. Satan doesn't want you offering sacrifices to God. Therefore, he begins using the same tactics that have worked on so many of God's children and stopped them from their God-given assignment. It surely worked on the Israelites because nowhere in chapter 5 of Exodus does it say they called on God. Quite the opposite—they approached Pharaoh and pleaded with him to stop the harsh abuse (Ex 5:15). This should be a lesson for us whenever we experience triggers from our journey back to Egypt. Whenever the devil invades your mind with thoughts or lies, it's time to pull out your weapons instead of panic.

The whole armor of God

If you weren't aware, let me be the first to tell you that there is a way to negate the strategies of the devil. Many of us are familiar with the armor of God in the Bible, yet we still struggle using our spiritual weapons. Ephesians 6:11 tells us this armor of God allows you to stand firm against *all* the devil's strategies. May I emphasize that it says *all?* Not *some.* Not only the strategies that come against you when you feel strong. That's right, even when you are at your weakest, this armor fights off all of Satan's strategies. Please, please let that soak in. Too many of us flee from our deep hurts because we can't take the pain. The problem is that we weren't meant to take the pain. You're not supposed to *always* be strong or be so tough that you can handle anything that comes your way. I am a huge believer in having grit, but when it comes to spiritual warfare, it's time to put down willpower and load up on your spiritual weapons. Christ came and shed His blood on the cross so you didn't have to bear the pain on your own. Decide today to approach your pain with a different mindset, one that says, "I am in agony, and my heart is grieving, but I stand on the truth that Christ bears my burdens" (Mt 11:28–30).

Accusations begin, and the enemy brings up your past and shoves it in your face. You think you're no good and that everything you've done is unforgivable. Your first line of defense should always be to go to God in prayer. Once you've prayed or during your prayer time, begin accessing your first two pieces of armor: the *belt of truth* and the *body armor of God's righteousness*. If someone told you that they flew to Mars, you'd laugh and think they were lying. Your reasoning would kick in, and all sorts of scientific truths would flood your mind, proving to you this was a lie. The same should happen when the enemy begins with his lies. You should shut the lies down with the truth. The truth is that you are a child of the most high God. The truth is that you made mistakes, but the blood of Christ possesses all power and has the ability to cleanse and purify you (1 Jn 1:7). The truth is that God is righteous, which indicates His goodness and perfection.

Your third piece of armor is shoes, which represent *peace* (Eph 6:15). This peace comes from the good news of the gospel—that is, Christ shed His blood so that you would be saved. It is already done, and there is nothing hell can do to stop or undo this.

Your fourth piece of armor is your *shield of faith*, which stops the fiery arrows of the devil (Eph 6:16). A little bit of faith goes a long way. You may not believe in yourself, but your faith in God can move mountains (Mt 17:20).

Your fifth and sixth pieces of armor are your *helmet of salvation* and the *sword of the Spirit: God's Word*.

Romans 10:9–10 tells us that if we confess with our mouths that Jesus is Lord and believe in our hearts that God raised Him from the dead, we'll be saved. Stand on this truth regarding your salvation. Don't let the enemy taunt you with false guilt, making you think you are going to hell because of your sins. God's Word is more powerful than lies. It is sharper than the sharpest two-edged sword and can cut between soul and spirit as well as between joint and marrow (Heb 4:12).

You don't need to memorize the whole Bible to unlock your armor. Begin with just a few scriptures that speak to your problem and recite them whenever you feel you're being attacked.

I'm not a people person

I want to remind you that people are not your problem (Eph 6:12). This may sound absurd because all the problems we face seem to come from people. However, this is another lie of the enemy we need to expose. Some of us hate being around people and consider ourselves a loner. We think people are what's wrong with the world and take pride in having no friends or letting anyone close to us. It is okay to enjoy alone time, but when God has an assignment for you, it will involve people. And depending on your gift, there may be a lot of people you're destined to help! Don't shut the pages and toss the book across the room. Hear me out. You need to begin seeing people as Christ sees them, not how the devil sees them. Satan sees people as a problem, and the solution is to get rid of them. Christ sees people through the eyes of a shepherd. He understands we have shortcomings and need a lot of grace. The Bible poses a question: "If we don't love people we can see, how can we love God, whom we cannot see?" (1 Jn 4:20). The answer is you can't. There is no wall between your love for others and your love for God. They spill over into each other. You cannot have both hate and love in your heart. With that being said, I understand we can feel love for God and truly want to serve Him but struggle with hatred for another person. However, the hate and love will be at war with each other, and one has to win. It's just as the Bible says: you cannot love God and money because you'll love one and hate the other (Mt 6:24). Eventually, you'll yield and let the love of God drown out the hate, or you'll choose hate over God.

For most of us, going back to Egypt consists of forgiving those who have wronged us (or forgiving ourselves). We cannot go back to Egypt, then to the Promised Land until we have forgiven. We also cannot expect the Lord to forgive us if we cannot forgive others (Mt 6:14). Forgiveness is an action step you take that feeds your inner healing. When you forgive someone, you are surrendering to God and allowing Him to enter your heart. It doesn't mean you are weak—quite the contrary as it takes someone with courage to forgive. It doesn't mean all your ill feelings will go away either. In fact, you will need to pray often regarding your ill feelings so that you can fully release them. We can get confused about whether we've forgiven someone when we still feel the same feelings we felt before we forgave them. To make matters more complicated, if you google the definition of *forgive*, it will speak to feelings toward someone. Sometimes I *feel* like I'm going to lose my cool with my children and strangle them. However, I have never manifested this thought or even come close to strangling my children. I love and adore them with all my heart, and that feeling came out of frustration. I know I am a great mother, and my children are blessed to have someone who would jump in front of a bullet for them. I don't confuse my momentary feeling of frustration with the fact that I love my children. Instead, I pray through my frustration and allow God to work on me. It's no different from forgiving someone. Forgive, then work through the feelings.

If you start to understand the difference between forgiveness and feelings, it will help speed up the process of forgiveness. This is because you won't have to go back and forth with yourself or feel guilty because you haven't forgiven them. You'll know the truth and can embrace that you're human and that it will take you time to let go of your ill feelings. Changing our perspective on people can be a challenge, but if you remind yourself that Satan is the root cause of all destruction, you'll begin to see the root cause of destruction in others. Learning this truth through the Word of God will help you begin seeing the hurt in others. You'll gain compassion for them and find yourself praying for their healing.

Please note that this is not a license to excuse someone's behavior. We need to set boundaries and refuse to let others abuse or misuse us. We can do so, however, with grace and love. I end with Ephesians 4 where it begins with the apostle Paul begging us to lead a life worthy of our calling because we are called by God.

He tells us to be humble, gentle, and patient and make allowance for one another's faults because of our *love*.

Testimony time

I mentioned in the last chapter that my going back to Egypt included forgiving those who had hurt me. Forgiving was just one part, however, since I needed to learn how to love people, or I would continue being offended by the actions of others. I had the mindset that people were a problem. I found myself ready to explode with outbursts of anger, and the trigger was the actions of others. But as I allowed God to enter my heart, I realized that if I didn't learn to love others, I could not fulfill the assignment God had for me.

Whenever God has called you, know that it will include others. There is no escaping people. Yes, many have hurt us, but there are many others out there who need our testimony. They, too, need to learn how to forgive and rise above generational curses so they can help others.

I won't lie and say loving people is easy. We're human, and as Paul said, "I don't really understand myself, for I want to do what is right, but I don't do it. Instead, I do what I hate" (Rom 7:15). Whenever I struggle with loving others, I go to God's Word because I know what I feel at the moment does not come from God. I don't try to pretend to love people. Instead, I read Ephesians 4 to remind myself of God's Word. I acknowledge my shortcomings, repent, then move forward. I deploy the whole armor of God and agree with the Spirit that I must love. Most importantly, I remind myself that I don't need to be perfect for God to use me. Any pain that I feel because of my interactions with others will just be used by God. I take pride that God wastes nothing, and He allows me to feel pain so I cling to Him, be open to His voice, and soften my heart so I can love.

Chapter 6

Don't Turn Back

*So Moses told the people of Israel what the Lord had
said, but they refused to listen anymore. They had become
too discouraged by the brutality of their slavery.*
—Ex 6:9 (NLT)

Promises

ONE OF THE THINGS I adore about the Father is that He takes time to make promises to His children, then continues to remind them of those promises. Throughout the book of Exodus (or the Bible, for that matter) God continues to remind His children who He is and what He will do for them. If you are a parent, you know that sometimes you'll make a promise to your child, and you better get to it fast because they won't let you forget. It's interesting how children seem not to listen to a word you're saying until they hear key words like *candy* or *ice cream*. Then they're all ears, and they're going to hold you to your promises. It can be quite frustrating when you have made a promise to your child, made all the plans to execute, and have full intentions of making it happen, but they question if or when you're going to do it for them. It can almost be offensive with small children because they have no ability to take care of themselves yet question if you're going to do what you said you're going to do. I believe God feels the same with us. He makes a promise to us, works everything out with full intentions of carrying out His promise, has supreme power, and can do anything, yet we question if He's going to do it or His timing. We see in chapter 6 of Exodus that God does not forget His covenant. God is itching to carry out His promises in your life.

Another thing I adore about the Father is that He uniquely does something for each of us. He treats us special, and when we commit our lives to Him, we can be sure that He has something reserved for just us. It can be a beautiful house, business territory, a new church building, or an invention. It's not just material things either; it can be a friendship, a spouse, an idea, or the very thing this book is about: *an assignment.* God freely gives His love to each one of us; that isn't something He reserves for a certain group of people. But God does have a way of taking care of us in a way that makes us feel important. I love how God reveals Himself as Yahweh to Moses, something He did not do with Abraham, Isaac, or Jacob (Ex 6:3). It just proves that we can have a special encounter with God and that it produces greatness in us but doesn't rob someone else of their greatness. Each person in the Bible has his or her own story of their unique encounter with God. Moses had a special place with God, but so did Abraham. Paul had a special place with God, but so did Peter.

We live in a society that says we must work to be the best. We should be better, work harder, become smarter, and look prettier. It's no wonder why we have such deep insecurity and low self-esteem. Instead of having a community mindset, it's every man for himself, and we end up leaving so many people behind. The Bible says to pay careful attention to your own work, then you'll be satisfied with doing well and won't need to compare yourself to anyone else (Gal 6:4).

The herd mentality

Sometimes, when God gives you an assignment, you'll quickly realize why when you see the resistance in others. Moses went back to the Israelites to remind them of God's promises, but they refused to listen because circumstances got harder (Ex 6:9). It is clear that Moses was chosen for this assignment because he hadn't endured the hardship of slavery the Israelites did. He had a different mindset, and God wanted to use that. The same is true for us; God sees something in us that's different and wants to use it. However, if we're not careful, we'll lose what's unique about us and pick up the herd mentality. I'm sure there were some Israelites who wanted to believe Moses, but the herd mentality ruled, and they didn't speak up.

Moses objected the Lord, saying his own people would not listen to him (Ex 6:12). Listen, there will be people who are depressed, soul tied, discouraged, and can't perceive the vision you have laid out. Don't let it stop you from being obedient to God! Notice that the Bible says, "The Lord *commanded* Moses and Aaron" (Ex 6:13; emphasis added). This isn't just about your assignment; it's about being obedient to the command of the Lord. It doesn't matter how good your excuses are. God will not let you out of what He's called you to do. Resist adopting the herd mentality and let God change your thinking so He can accomplish great things in you. If you recognize that you already have the herd mentality, don't lose hope. God still wants to use you! You just need to surrender to Him and let Him work on the renewing of your mind through His Word and pouring His wisdom into you.

Testimony time

Just like Moses, I've spent time in "Midian"—not physically but figuratively, of course. God had to isolate me from those who had no intention of serving Him and uproot the herd mentality in me. There were a lot of things I desired for my life including wealth. In fact, I wanted to be wealthy more than I wanted to serve God. I wasn't aware of this until I got closer and closer to God, however. He helped me realize there is a lot of brokenness in the world and that there are many people chasing things before God. But before God could use me to bring a revelation, He had to change me first. I learned what it means to be a woman after God's own heart. In my most intimate moments with God, I've surrendered my all to Him, leaving nothing off the table. Even in areas where I was afraid to let go, I acknowledged it and still pleaded that the Lord would have His way. I realized that in order for the Lord to use me, it is my obligation to let Him do what needs to be done in me. It is my inspiration in writing this book. I'm able to write with conviction and through experience because I know what it's like to have a herd mentality but break through and become fully free. I can't say I'm perfect because nobody is.

At the time of writing this book, God has reminded me that there should never be a limit to how much we love because God doesn't limit His love for us. Sometimes I get angry or frustrated with the herd mentality in others. When that happens, I have to quiet my mind and open my heart to listen to God. I remind myself not to be hypocritical and recognize that I, too, am a work in progress. I don't have to be perfect. I rest in knowing that I have allowed God to work in and through me. He never fails me either because I begin to see progress in my life. He is my hope and salvation, and He is the reason I fight.

It is my prayer and hope that you will read this book with conviction and that you will recognize that it's not until you allow Him full access that you'll receive your healing and fulfill your God-given assignment. Sometimes you'll question why things are so chaotic in your life, and you'll be ready to give up. The promises of God won't come easily because the devil is waiting to sabotage as much as he can so you don't receive these promises. Don't become like the Israelites, moaning, groaning, and losing faith in our Father. Recognize the attack and implement the weapons we talked about in the last chapter. We need to adopt a kingdom mindset and let go of the worldly one. We need to stop putting things before God and place Him back on the throne of our hearts. We need to honor Him in everything we do and recognize that He is our Lord and that without Him, we are nothing, but with Him, we are everything.

Chapter 7

Discovering Your New Life

Then the Lord said to Moses, "Pay close attention to this. I will make you seem like God to Pharaoh, and your brother, Aaron, will be your prophet."
                                                    —Ex 7:1 (NLT)

#MakeHisNameFamous

ONE OF THE THINGS THAT will help give you hope when you go back to Egypt is focusing on the promises of God. Yes, I mean the Word of God but also the personal promises God makes to us. For example, God told Moses He would make him seem like God to Pharaoh (Ex 7:1). This was a promise God made exclusively to Moses, and it had nothing to do with idolatry and everything to do with the greatness God was going to produce in Moses's life. We need to learn how to crave what God said He's going to do and let it be fuel to fight when we question if it's worth going back to Egypt. God has an interest in spreading your name because you are His mouthpiece. It's your opportunity to represent Him and truly honor Him before those who show interest in what you're trying to accomplish. It is not about your will but God's will. It's not about being famous or having a massive following but about God creating a platform for you so you can bring people to Christ.

The mistake many people make is taking their God-given gifts, talents, and abilities to the world for self-motivated reasons and leading people astray. God wants to make us great among men, but our focus shouldn't be on being popular but putting Christ first. Ultimately, this should give you hope because wherever you feel your life is lacking, God can and will use you. His desire is for you to live in the fullness of peace, having forgiven all who've wronged you as well as having been healed from past hurts and mistakes, delivered from sin, grounded in your identity in Christ, and confident that He can transform your life. Did you catch that?

It is possible to be so jacked up, but God changes you into a completely different person. You can live the beautiful life that God desires for you to live. Stop believing the lies of the enemy, especially the one that says that this living hell is it for you. The Bible says that anyone belonging to Christ has become a new person; the old life is dead and gone (2 Cor 5:17). I encourage you to read through 2 Corinthians 5 so you can see what God's Word says about our new life and responsibility to reconcile people back to him.

Counterfeits

God makes it clear to Moses and Aaron that Pharaoh will refuse to listen but that it's an opportunity for God to perform miraculous signs and wonders in Egypt (Ex 7:3). Ultimately, those who are stubborn and refuse to obey the command of the Lord will know at the end of the day that He is El Shaddai and that there is no other like Him. Still, people refuse to acknowledge the Lord and even partake in Satan's plot against God's people. They are wolves in sheep's clothing promoting a false sense of happiness. They'll dress happiness up to draw you in and take you further away from Christ. They'll tell you that love is love, yet the Bible says God is love (1 Jn 4:8). It is important that we not cling to a false sense of hope and build our house on the rock (Mt 24:27). The power of God will always reign and rule. Even Pharaoh's wise men and sorcerers could not outperform the miracles of God (Ex 7:11–12).

Chapters 7 through 11 of Exodus consist of many plagues against Egypt because of their wickedness. These verses show exactly the type of counterfeit that still tries to consume our world today. Let's not put God in the same category as the world because the world belongs to Him, so whatever good you think you see, if Christ is not at its foundation, it is false. There is only one true God, and there is only one way to receive salvation (1 Kgs 8:60, Rom 10:9–10).

There will always be counterfeit to God's truth, so we must pray for discernment. We also need to understand that discernment comes from knowing the Word of God (i.e., Scripture). You cannot discern if something is not Christlike until you understand God's nature, but to understand God's nature, you must spend time in His Word. If we are going to fulfill our God-given assignment, then we must have discernment, or we'll get pulled offtrack by counterfeits. We'll settle for the wise men and sorcerers instead of the power of the Spirit. We'll build our house on sinking sand and never make it to our Promised Land. Jesus warned us that our eye is the lamp that provides light for the body. When your eye is unhealthy, your whole body is filled with darkness, and how deep that darkness is if you think it's the light (Mt 6:22–23).

Testimony Time

As with Moses, God has made personal promises to me. But also like Moses, He never gives me the full picture, but I trust Him anyways. In my private time with God, I have learned to hear from His spirit to know if God is the one who has spoken. I always approach carefully what I've heard, analyzing if Christ is at the center and if it promotes the good of His children. I have also learned how to quickly recognize if I've become self-motivated and put my will before God's. This is all important because on my journey to my Promised Land, I learned that God has trusted me to represent Him with truth and love. It hurts my heart to see so many led astray by false prophecy and counterfeits. I have a duty to be honest, have integrity, and love God's children, teaching them only the truth of God's Word. I do it with gladness in my heart because God has given me glimpses into my future. He's shown me places He will take me and how He'll use me to impact the world and revealed to me how my obedience will bring blessings on my life and my family. I crave the promises of God and have become forever indebted to Him.

It's crazy to look back at the person I was and see how I've become so in love with Christ and committed. All because I let Him have His way in my life, in return, I can receive the promises of God. I can't say I've "arrived," but I can definitely say I'm well on my way. If you had told me five years ago that I'd be where I am today, I wouldn't believe you. I have truly seen God transform my life and use me in great ways. I own who I am in my new life, and it is my prayer that this testimony inspires you to fight for the future God has for you.

Chapter 8

Untouched

For the Lord will pass through the land to strike down the Egyptians. But when he sees the blood on the top and sides of the doorframe, the Lord will pass over your home. He will not permit his death angel to enter your house and strike you down.
—Ex 12:23 (NLT)

Accepting the truth

I PROPHETICALLY DECLARE TO YOU TODAY that you and your household cannot be touched because you are covered with the blood of Jesus Christ. It is time to take back all that has been stolen from you so that you can fulfill your God-given assignment. This is what the story of Moses and the Israelites represents—allowing God to deliver us from slavery and give us the life He has designed for us. Our minds have been enslaved, but that changes *today*. Won't you stand in agreement with me and not lie down and die? Won't you cling to God's Word and believe Him over the lies of the enemy? For those of you who are struggling with your past, feel like you've done something that God just cannot forgive, and won't accept that God wants to use you, let me share this dream God gave me.

I dreamt that a father was sexually abusing his daughter. I did not catch him in the act, but I could sense it in the spirit. We were at a gas station, getting ready to fill the gas tank. I was sitting in the passenger seat of a white van, and the man and his daughter got out of the car to go pump the gas. The Holy Spirit told me to look into the rearview mirror, and as I looked up, I could see him harassing her. It broke my heart. There were two others with me, and they were in the back seat of the van and could see what he was doing. The daughter came back into the car, sitting in the back seat, next to the others, and I could see the hurt in her eyes. The father climbed back into the driver's seat, and I, too, could see the hurt in his eyes.

The other passengers began persecuting him for what he had done (this represents Satan, the accuser). He lashed out back at them, and there was chaos between them. I looked over at him, grabbed his hand, and began to prophesy to him. I told him that God loved him and wanted to forgive him but that he needed to stop his sin and surrender. I reminded him that God loved him even in spite of this wicked act but that nothing would change unless He let God in. Well, what about the daughter? I hear you. She was definitely a victim in such a wicked act, but she wasn't the only victim.

I am in no way excusing the father's actions. I am just accepting the truth that people do things out of hurt. I know what it feels like to be violated as a child and be forced to do things no child should have to do. But I'd rather forgive my abuser and live in the fullness of Christ than let it consume me. The truth is that we all fall short of the glory of God, and we all need Him. Until we can accept that God loves us and can forgive us, the cycle will continue to repeat itself.

Some of the most loved stories in the Bible are about people who loved God and did what God asked of them. They had a heart for the Lord and were willing to lay down their lives for His just cause. But almost all of them had done something that we would consider unforgivable. Moses murdered an Egyptian. Paul persecuted the Christians of the first-century church. King David committed adultery and murder. Abram had a baby with his wife Sarai's Egyptian servant, Hagar. Peter denied He knew Jesus. Shall I keep going?

The Bible says we should not abuse grace, so in no way am I suggesting we do what we want because we'll be forgiven (Rom 6:15–16). I am saying, however, that we need to accept this grace and understand the truth that we are forgiven so we can rise up and begin to plead the blood of Jesus over our lives. We *must* do this in order to fulfill the assignment that God has for us. We cannot move forward to our Promised Land until we understand this. If we are not grounded in what God's Word says about being forgiven and who we are in Christ, we'll be moved by false teachings and won't make it to the Promised Land (Eph 4:14). It doesn't matter that you were once a slave like the Israelites. Your past does not define you. The truth is that when you live in obedience, you are untouched. We see this with the Israelites who followed God's instructions and put blood on their doorframes (Ex 12:23). Because of their obedience, the death angel passed over their homes, and their families were safe.

Testimony time

There was a time in my life where I could not accept that God had forgiven me for watching pornography and participating in premarital sex. It's intriguing how when you live apart from Christ, you indulge in sin with no remorse. But the moment you begin surrendering, condemnation seeps in, and you can't see how God could forgive you. Satan makes you feel like you don't deserve forgiveness and as if God is displeased with you. This is false guilt. The problem with false guilt is that it holds you to your past, and you'll end up having relapses of old behavior. However, I learned about false guilt through counseling and reading *The Search for Significance: Seeing Your True Worth through God's Eyes* by Robert S. McGee.

You see, it was my deep desire to live for Christ that drove me to want answers. I had a heart for Jesus and no longer wanted to live in sin, and Satan knew this. He tried to confuse my mind with false guilt so I would not accept the authority I had in Christ. He knew that once I knew the truth, hell would lose any control it had over my life. Hell knew I was a weapon not to be unleashed because once unleashed, there was no power that could stop me.

I share this with you in the hope that you'll begin taking back what's yours. Get tired of false guilt and the lies that have been controlling you for so long. Yes, there may be people who will never forgive you and always hold your past against you. All you can do is pray for them and move forward into your Promised Land. But make a commitment to live in obedience and accept the truth of God's Word.

Chapter 9

Wisdom for the Wise

*You're going to wear yourself out—and the people, too. This
job is too heavy a burden for you to handle all by yourself.*
—Ex 18:18 (NLT)

Food for thought

Let's switch gears as we prepare to discuss being in the
Promised Land. I've gone through Exodus and highlighted some
principles that we can apply to our lives. This list is not all-inclu-
sive, and if you've ever read the Bible, you know there is an endless
amount of revelations in every passage. If you've gotten additional
principles from reading through Exodus or any part of Scripture,
for that matter, great. But I'd like to share with you some of what I
have discovered from the book of Exodus:

- *Train a child up.* Dedicate your children to the Lord. I
  cannot express this enough. The enemy is working over-
  time to devour our children, so we must lead them in
  the way they should go. Your children are your legacy.
  There is no greater success than bringing your children
  to Christ, which is all the more reason to seek the help.
  You need to heal because your children need you. They

don't just need to see the good either. It's lovely to speak of the goodness of the Lord and celebrate our wins, but we must show our children how the Lord gets us through trials as well. The Israelites were instructed to remember the day they left Egypt forever (Ex 13). We need to do the same and continue to celebrate this time so our children can witness the goodness of our Savior in their own homes.

- *God will make a way.* I believe this phrase has become a cliché: "God will make a way." Let's take a moment and think about what this is saying. Will God *find* a way? No, that's not right. Will God *figure* out a way? That's not it either. God will *make* a way. We serve the same God who parted the Red Sea (Ex 14:21). We have forgotten that our Lord is limitless and that all things are possible to those who believe (Mk 9:23). We may not see how it will work out, but we need to believe that God can and will make a way. Let's be clear: our belief isn't what makes something possible for God. Our belief, however, activates His sovereign power in our lives. Don't focus on what you can't do. Instead, focus on what God can do.

- *Worship is your weapon.* Moses and the Israelites sang a beautiful song of deliverance in Exodus 15. We, too, can sing our psalms of worship to the Lord, and we should do this regularly, not just during times of celebration. The Bible says to "enter into his gates with thanksgiving, and into His courts with praise: be thankful unto him, and bless his name" (Ps 100:4) Do not underestimate the power of your worship because it brings you into the very presence of God. If you are struggling to worship because you feel beaten down, I encourage you to read and meditate on Psalm 34. Though we get weary, God's Word has a way of penetrating our hearts.

- *God will provide.* Not only will He make a way, but also, He will provide. If we're not careful, we will begin complaining, as the Israelites did in the wilderness because they were not confident that God would provide (Ex 16:3). Yet in His undeserved mercy, He poured down fresh manna and quail from heaven. Do you believe God wants to take care of you? If not, today I want to tell you that God wants to supply all your needs (Phil 4:19). He cares about you deeply, and just as any loving father, He wants to provide for you and protect you.

- *Take wise advice.* Moses, no doubt, had wisdom. For starters, he had the Almighty on his side. He was there with him every step of the way. However, we see in the Bible that God used Jethro to give Moses some wise advice on how he should lead the Israelites (Ex 18). Moses gladly took this advice and became a better leader. You don't have to know it all, and, in fact, you will never know it all no matter how much wisdom God gives you. Be sure to seek godly counsel from your elders or those who have more experience in an area than you. God uses others to speak to us, and you can be sure that if the advice you receive comes from God, it will resonate with your spirit.

- *God is your friend.* The Lord revealed Himself to Moses at Sinai (Ex 19). It wasn't the last time Moses experienced this closeness with God either. They were friends and often spoke one-on-one (Ex 33:11). God is our provider, our comforter and so much more including our friend. You truly have a friend in Jesus. You are never alone and you have someone who will always understand you and want what's best for you. This is a *true* friend. Take comfort in knowing your friendship will never change and God will reveal who He is through Christ.

- *Follow God's instructions.* There's a reason God gives us instructions. Sometimes we take God's instructions as optional or we even disagree with what He's saying because we don't understand. I have personally experienced debating with God because I didn't understand. However, I've learned that God does not negotiate. He gives you instructions for a reason and that reason is because He knows what's best for you. He knows the outcome. He knows what you'll experience in the future. He knows it all. We'll get exhausted very quickly trying to do things our own way and not God's way. This will distract us from our assignment and only cause stress and fatigue. It's best we listen to what God is asking us to do, else we risk dying in the wilderness (metaphorically of course) as the Israelites who never made it into the Promised Land. God gave many instructions throughout the book of Exodus and as you read through them, you will quickly find out that there are consequences to disobedience. Save yourself the time, trouble, and excuses and begin to listen to God today.

Testimony time

One of my favorite stories in the Bible is from 1 Kings 3 when God asked Solomon what he wanted. God was ready to give Solomon whatever he asked for. Solomon did not ask for riches or fame, but he asked God for wisdom to help others. I've learned that no matter how close I get to God, I am still human and fall short. Rather than be discouraged, I take pride in knowing that true wisdom comes only from God (Prv 2:6). I make it a habit to ask God for His wisdom because I recognize that apart from it, I can accomplish nothing. I pray that you've seen this wisdom and understanding in the pages you've read thus far. As you move toward your own Promised Land, it's crucial that you seek the wisdom of the God, or else you risk ending up back in Egypt.

Chapter 10

The Promised Land

*Be strong and courageous, for you are the one who
will lead these people to possess all the land I swore
to their ancestors I would give them.*

—Jo 1:6 (NLT)

What will it be?

WE'VE TALKED A LOT ABOUT going back to Egypt, but now it's time to shift our focus to heading into the Promised Land. While going back to Egypt is critical for healing and moving into our God-given assignment, it's important that we don't get stuck in the past. It would be a tragedy to begin the healing process but become so focused on those who've wronged us or our mistakes and never move forward, especially since going back to Egypt was never about our past to begin with but about resolving past issues to cultivate a better future. Unfortunately, the Israelites let this happen to them and never made it into the Promised Land. It was Joshua, Caleb, and the descendants of the Israelites who made it as their ancestors (the Israelite slaves who left Egypt) died in the wilderness. They never allowed Egypt to leave their hearts so never inherited the full promises of God. Yes, they left Egypt. Yes, they witnessed the hand of God in their lives. Yes, they walked through the Red Sea. All these are wonderful, but they only reflect the goodness of God, not their full obedience or faith. Will you let this happen to you, or will you decide to let God fully deliver you from Egypt? Will you be the one that God speaks to, as He did with Joshua (Jo 1:1)? The one He uses to help impact generations? The one who decides that it's better to live a fulfilled life in Christ than cling to lies and the pain of the past? The one who fights for the promises of God and will trust God's assignment for them?

You may feel like God won't use you until you've become a better person, until you've fully transformed and become who you were destined to be. Don't make this mistake because God begins using you the day you say yes to Him. He did this with Moses, remember? When Moses did what God asked, the transformation from the old life to the new one began, and he grew along the way. Do as Moses did; follow God's instruction and allow Him to transform you along the journey.

I caution you not to get stuck on not knowing your purpose. Many of us are paralyzed by not knowing our purpose, and it's because we are confused between purpose and assignment. If you are alive today, then your purpose is to receive salvation (Rom 9:10), be reconciled back to Christ, and help reconcile others back to Christ (2 Cor 5:18–20). That's it. We all have the same purpose for being born on this earth. Our assignment, on the other hand, is unique to us all. That being said, our assignment will fulfill our purpose because whatever God calls us to do will impact others and bring them to know their Savior. And if you have a testimony, your assignment most likely includes you sharing that testimony with others.

Ultimately, we shouldn't get stuck on not knowing what the future holds when we know the one who holds the future. Keep your mind on moving into the Promised Land and celebrate minor accomplishments throughout the journey. This will help keep you motivated and focused on what's in front of you instead of your past life. Celebrate that you forgave someone or that you said yes to God. Celebrate that you said no to what displeases God and decided to follow His will instead. Celebrate the renewing of your mind or that you've changed your perspective. Celebrate that you're willing to let God use you to end the cycles that have consumed your family for generations. It doesn't matter how small it may seem. Celebrate everything God does in your life because it's the small things that add up to radical change. Don't make the mistakes of the Israelites who didn't make it into Egypt because they focused on the wrong in their life. Instead, focus on what God is doing, will do, and is going to do in your life. This is a sure way to make it into the Promised Land.

It's worth mentioning that sometimes we are tempted to see what the world says about success. There are, no doubt, some great tools out there, but don't forget that Christ is the foundation of all success. God gave Joshua a charge to study the book of instructions Moses gave him (Jo 1:7–8). Only then would he prosper and succeed in all he did. Joshua obeyed the Lord's command, and he and the next generation of Israelites made it into the Promised Land because of it. The same is true for us; we must prioritize Bible study in our lives because God's Word is the root of our success and what gets us into the Promised Land. It is our GPS of life. If we don't have our GPS, Satan will continue to detour us in the wilderness. But if we do as Joshua did, we are guaranteed success. I don't just mean being successful with material things and status. It's success in all we do, including being a good spouse and parent, living a godly life, and so much more. We'll surely make some mistakes along the way, but our GPS will reroute us back onto the correct way to the Promised Land.

Beware not to use the Bible as manipulation to get whatever you want. God's Word will be of no use to you if you use it for self-motivated reasons.

Heaven on earth

Might I say it's lovely in the Promised Land? It truly is heaven on earth. It's amazing how many people don't understand what the fullness of life is. We believe that if we have riches or fame, then we've truly lived, but that just isn't true. The truth is this life is temporary, but we don't have to wait until we die to experience heaven. What does heaven on earth look or feel like? It's when you put God first, and your relationship with Him grows deeper and deeper each day. You feel His presence, and without a doubt, you know there is a God because you recognize His supernatural tendencies, both through your life and all around you. You're in tune with His spirit, which captivates you and helps you connect with God. Your spiritual eyes open, and the world begins to look different; you now recognize many are running around, hopeless, looking for fulfillment in things and not Christ. You want to help them. You have a burning desire to live like Christ, but in no way do you limit what Christ can do in your life. You recognize that you serve a supernatural Father, so you say yes to whatever it is He asks of you. Yes, sometimes you'll get scared, but you remind yourself who and whose you are, so you never let being scared stop you from what God has called you to. You have no fear of Satan and his tactics, and in fact, he fears you because you've woken up from the deep sleep he put you in. You are a force to be reckoned with; nothing or no one can stop you. It's not arrogance or cockiness. In fact, you remain humble because you know you would be nothing without Christ. You begin to recognize that you are talented and gifted and no longer think badly about yourself. In fact, you are confident because you know who you are in Christ. You say, "Use me, God," and He does just that.

I believe heaven on earth isn't just spiritual. God made many promises in the Bible, indicating He also cares about our physical needs. The Bible tells us not to worry about *anything* but instead pray about everything, tell God what we need, and thank Him for all He has done (Phil 4:6). What is it that you need? Are you ready for a spouse? Maybe you're already married, and you want God to transform your marriage so that it pleases him. Do you want children? Better health? A new car or house? Do you want to pay off all your debt, or do you want to start a business? Do you want more money in general, or do you want to travel? Whatever you want, you can ask God for. We don't have to limit heaven on earth. God is a provider and He knows we have physical needs. As long as we don't put things before God, it's perfectly fine to dream big and desire more for your life.

Don't let false guilt or the fear of appearing greedy or worldly prevent you from asking God for what you need. Living in lack is not God's desire for your life, and He certainly wants to provide for all your needs. Think of what it's like to be a parent, especially for young children. We provide shelter, food, clothing, entertainment, assistance, and anything else our children need. We do not limit taking care of our child to just basic shelter, food, and clothing, but we recognize they have other needs we need to meet. Our children do not limit what they ask us for because they know we're their providers and take care of them. It would break our hearts if our children didn't trust us enough to provide for them and instead asked a stranger to meet their needs. This is true with God. Our Father doesn't want us asking the world for wealth or material things. In fact, when God is the one who provides material things, He does it in such a way that truly blesses us. He knows when you're ready to receive what you've asked for and matures you in such a way that when you receive, you are full of gratitude. There are no strings attached either. He blesses us from His unlimited resources and doesn't enslave us to do things the world requires us to do.

There is such a thing as a joyful life. I'll go out on a limb here and say that I believe our lives can be perfect. Why? Because we serve a perfect God. It doesn't mean we should become narcissists or think of ourselves as perfect; that's *not* what I'm saying. I mean that no matter what happens in our lives, the perfect will of God will always show itself. So no matter how bad things may seem, we have faith, hope, and love, which last forever (1 Cor 13:13). This is a foreign concept to many of us because things just look so dark in our lives. I'm not making a promise that things will never go dark in your life. In fact, they sometimes will. The Bible says it rains on both the unjust and just (Mt 5:45). This means that no matter who or where you are, you will experience the aches and pains of life. Remember the story of Job, who lost everything, including all his possessions, health, and children? His story shows us that things do go dark for God's children but that it's temporary when we are committed to the Lord. I know what it's like to feel depression and be a Christian. In that time of depression, however, I clung tight to faith, hope, and love, and depression lost its sting. When I came out, I came out on top, fully equipped and ready to smack the devil in his face!

No one is exempt; we all experience pain. So choose your pain wisely! Will it be the pain of the world? The pain of refusing to confront your issues head-on? The pain of living dormant and allowing the waves of life to take you wherever? Or will your pain be from fighting for your freedom? Will you allow God to renew your mind and show you the truth? Will you say yes to the assignment God has for you? Take back what is yours! Get all the help you need and pray to God earnestly to show you the way. Use discernment and take the time you need to heal. Do whatever it is you need to do to leave Egypt and enter into the Promised Land.

> Awake, O sleeper, rise up from the dead, and
> Christ will give you light. (Eph 5:14)

Don't run from the light that Christ wants to shed on your life. Allow Him to wake you up and out of your sleep and focus on His promises.

Testimony time

I can honestly say I have fully healed from the pain of my past. Going back to Egypt was hard. I had to deal with triggers and overcome false guilt. There were times I wanted to give up because I felt I could not bear the pain. At times I felt like what God was asking me to do was too much and that I could not handle it. I had to learn how to forgive myself, especially when I had relapses and fell back into old behavior. I had to learn my identity in Christ and let go of who I used to be. I had to accept the truth of who I was in Christ so that God could have His way. I had to face the truth of generational cycles in my family, such as sexual abuse, and take back authority so it would not consume my children. I had to learn how to pray without ceasing and fight without quitting.

I have shared much of my personal life with you thus far, but if there is only one thing you can gain from my testimony, I hope it's that I would be nothing without Christ. He has made me who I am, and He has shown me what true freedom looks like. I pray that this book has brought light to the darkness and order to the chaos in your life. Continue to fail forward and forgive yourself whenever you make a mistake. I end with this prayer of surrender. Won't you pray with me so that God will have His way in your life?

Prayer of Surrender

Dear Father,

Thank You that Your love for me is so strong that nothing on earth, in hell, or in heaven can separate me from it (Rom 8:38). I give my life to You today. I surrender my will to You and say, "Let Thy will be done." Have Your way in my life, Father, for it is a living sacrifice, a pleasing aroma to You. I recognize that I have fallen short and am in need of a Savior. I pray that You give me the wisdom to understand that my weakness is where Your strength begins. I admit today that I am weak without you. I confess that I need You and want You to use me as an instrument in the body of Christ. I recognize that You have an assignment for me and want to use me to reconcile Your children back to You. Do it today, Lord. Give me the wisdom I need to press forward into Your will. Help me live in obedience to You so my family and I remain under your protection. Reveal to me past hurts I need to confront, people I need to forgive, and habits I need to let go of. I pray that You would arrest my tongue and move me to silence before You whenever I try to make excuses to run away from what You called me to.

Holy Spirit, I pray for Your peace and warmth. Speak to me and tell me what to do. I need Your guidance. I need Your help. Today I make the decision to let go of everything that does not belong to You. Give me the boldness I need to stand as a witness for Christ. Surround me with those who have a heart for You—those who are rooted in sound doctrine and seek to build Your kingdom.

I declare that I am free! Thank You, Lord, for all that You have done in my life. Amen.

About the Author

Melony Bell is an author, speaker, and founder of Simply Powerful Living, an organization dedicated to helping women through their inner healing journey. Passionate about rising above generational cycles, discovering identity, and healthy mindsets, Melony frequently shares free content on YouTube. Visit www.melonysimonebell.com for more information on workshops, speaking events, and more.